A Moment From Darkness

Kristie Cooper

BookLeaf Publishing

Presentation by *BookLeaf Publishing*

Web: www.bookleafpub.com

E-mail: info@bookleafpub.com

ISBN: 9789357211826

First edition 2023

DEDICATION

Richard Slater I owe you my life, you saved me and built my confidence back up when I was at my lowest. You have held my hand, made me believe in true love and realise I can do anything with you by my side.

To my Mum and Dad, thank you for loving, supporting and believing in me.

Rope

Your rope is too short, I am hanging for you.
Your noose is too tight, I can't breathe.
All the pushing is making me fall, pick me up
again.

My heart is unlovable.
It's been abused.
Cracked, broken and bleeding.
Just an empty feeling.

Your rope is too long, I'm not hanging for you.
Your noose is loosening, I can breathe.
All the pushing that made me fall, I've picked
myself up again.

My heart is unlovable.
Its been abused.
Cracked, broken and bleeding.
Just an empty feeling.

Your rope is frayed, I'm not hanging at all.
Your noose is gone, I am breathing.
All the pushing now, is me pushing myself.

My heart is unlovable.
It's been abused.

Cracked, broken and bleeding.
Just an empty feeling.

Rejection

Red is my blood as it gushes out my wound,
the pain is instant, I will be dead soon.
The slashes to both my wrists are not half as bad
as the wound within.
My heart is broken, surely no pain is deeper than
this,
as I reach for you destined for one last kiss.
I am rejected, for she is the one you want.
And still I sit here with blood gushing out my
wrists.

Unveiling The Monster

'Do you take this woman to be your wife?
To have and to hold,
through good times and bad.
For richer for poorer,
in sickness and in health.
To love and cherish always,
till death do you part?
I do.
Do you take this man to be your husband?
To have to rape and hold me down.
Steal the good and create the bad.
Spend the riches and make me poor.
Make me sick and ruin my mental health.
To hate and punish always,
till the final beating do we part.
I do.

Shadow

The shadow stood before me.
A light shines bright in my eyes.
The shadow feels cold as it moves towards me.
My heart is racing my body feels numb.
The shadow pulls me towards the light.
I struggle and close my eyes.
The shadow pushes me to the ground.
A stabbing pain shoots through my body.
The shadow weighing me down.
I fall into a deep abyss within my mind.
The shadow is gone.
So i stand and turn my back to the light.

1943

You set out on your life's grand adventure, little did you know,
your life would change forever with your first fatal blow.
War did not suit you, nor was it kind,
you were not to know then, it would destroy your mind
The nightmares and the screams they followed you home,
but you survived now you must make it on your own.
Your mates are gone, your wife doesn't understand,
you need to deal with this alone, after all you are a man.
Do not show your weakness, it's the least you can do,
throw back the brandy it may help you see this through.
Drowning in regrets wishing you had never crossed that sea,
where the demons were born back in 1943.

Falling

Sometimes I don't understand anything at all,
why if you love me do you always let me fall?
Why do i say the things i say,
to make everyone I love turn and walk away?
I used to think your home was my heart,
but as we grew older we drifted apart.
Was it me that changed and ruined it all,
or was it just time that made our love fall?

Felo-de-se

My eyelids slowly close,
as I gently fall asleep.
The demons from inside me,
take my soul to keep.

Forcible Violation

Blackness surrounds me,
so does pain.
He smothers me,
ties me up.
Whispers, quiet whispers.
The cold air dances in my ears.
Rush of pain,
deeper and deeper.
The pain sinks.
I am numb.
More whispers, quiet whispers.
A lone tear rolls down my cheek.
The pain sinks.
I am dead.

Dejection

Suicide is what I think of lying in my bed.
it's what goes on inside my damaged head.
There is no turning back once you've made up your mind,
there is no point looking behind.
Maybe it's the easy way out, maybe its for chickens,
I am not scared of death for my last few seconds.
My mind is blank as I draw back the knife,
as sinks through my heart, I think what is the point to life.

Night War

The nights are frightening,
as the darkness closes in.
It is eerie and still,
except for the gentle breeze that blows through the trees.
The trees stand like giant creatures,
with enormous arms reaching out, as if they could take you and crush you.
The nights are filled with all sorts of unearthly sounds,
you can hear your own heartbeat, as if it echoes through the jungle.
Frightened, ready to attack or be attacked at any moment,
your mind plays tricks on you.
The black stump in front of you grows into the shape of a man,
you draw your rifle ready to take aim.
The darkness has taken away your most important sense,
your ears now must become your eyes.
The sweat pours off your forehead and your hands begin to shake,
slowly you realise there was never anybody there.

It is evil and cruel that the fear never rests,
whether it is day or night.
The sun slowly glitters through the trees,
thank God you survived another night in hell.

Coercive Control

I am trapped I don't know what to do,
it is going to take everything I have to get away from you.
I can not live like this anymore,
my heart is broken, heavy and sore.
I have wasted so much of my life with you,
believing you would change and stop the abuse.
Sorry is always your favourite word,
beat me then apologise how absurd.
You have successfully isolated me and brought me down,
all my confidence is now no where to be found.
The beatings are always my fault,
so you do not see this is domestic assault.
Instead all you do is make me feel crazy,
that none of this would of happened if i wasn't so lazy.
If I just did what you wanted or done what you had said,
I wouldn't be sitting here with blood pouring out my head.
If i don't leave you now, my heart will be forever sad,
and i will leave this house in a body bag.

Kinsman Stalker

He hurts me you know,
he really does.
He tries to rape me you know,
he really does.
He sneaks into my room at night,
he really does.
He watches me sleep,
he really does
Why don't you make him stop,
do you really care.
This is my space,
do you really care.
why is he welcome?
do you really care
I need help,
do you really care.
He really hurts me.

Ice Baby

You cheated on me,
She took our love.
She took my trust.
She took the money.
She left me beaten and bruised.
She took our time.
She took my dreams.
She took the house.
Dirty crack pipe.

Nefarious Mortal

Brutality your disclosure.
Tongue your deadly tool.
Aggression psyche.
Hands give voice.
Belligerent disposition.
Weapons award submission.
Hostile epitome.
Isolation gives control.
Nefarious mortal.

InstitutionaLIES

Conform to the power,
Obedient disciple.
Believe the lies,
Social experiment.
Consume the poison,
Devour some more.
Abstain from life,
Seclude in solitude.
Faculty rules,
Dictatorship incognito.
Suppress freedom.
Conceal candor,
Stifle existence.
Aeon Grippe.
It is a new world.

Mother

Screaming in your sleep,
crying wasn't uncommon.
You would yell out for your mother in the night,
you all wanted your mothers.
Grown men screaming out for their mothers,
it was cruel and disturbing.
Mothers have a way of making their children
feel safe,
but your mother is half a world away.
You are no longer a child,
and you are no longer safe.
All you have is your comrades,
your fear and your trepidation.
The terror of combat bonding men,
in a way the word brother only partially
encapsulates.
You became each other's mother,
sharing the commitment to safe guard each
others lives.
Just as a mother would,
a non negotiable pact.
You would sacrifice your life for your brother,
just as a mother would for her child.

Existence

Infinite time.
Passing expeditiously.
Ascending sun.
Rhythmic contraction.
Terminal life.

Trash And Treasure

You saw me,
you did not see me.
You heard me,
you did not listen to me.
You touched me,
you did not feel me.
He saw me,
he seen me.
He heard me,
he listened to me.
He touched me,
he felt me.

Foolish Love

All the times I have fallen in love,
I have been fooled.
All the times someone has fallen in love with
me,
I have fooled them.
I have never loved someone who loves me.
and no one I loved has ever loved me.

Downfall

I have done some things in my life I regret,
I can not seem to move on nor can I forget.
My life has sunk way down below,
I have hit the bottom with no where to go.
I keep trying, but things get worse,
I feel like my life is under a curse.
my depression and anxiety just wont go away,
I find it hard to face every day.
The harder I try the worse I do,
Why am I me, why can't I be like you?

From A Moment In Darkness

From a moment in darkness,
to a place of light.
Time circles the clock face.
The sun rises.
The moon phases.
Shadows change,
daylight shade.
From a moment in darkness,
to a brilliant illumination.
The earth orbits the sun.
The water flows.
The rain falls.
Dissipating storms,
rainbows magnify.
From a moment in darkness,
to a radiant self.
Follow the north star.
The dreams institution.
The demon buried.
Infinite cosmic,
matrix life.
From a moment in darkness,
to a lustrous entity.

www.ingramcontent.com/pod-product-compliance
Lightning Source LLC
Chambersburg PA
CBHW051719130826
49812CB00034B/1257
9789357211826